Count the things in each row. Write the matching number next to each group of things.

Count and add. Write the number in each box.

Count how many .

How many more are coming?

Write how many in all.

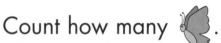

Count how many 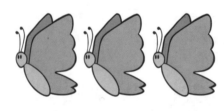.

How many more are coming?

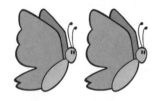

Write how many in all.

Count and add. Write the number in each box.

Count how many .

How many more are coming?

Write how many in all.

Count how many .

How many more are coming?

Write how many in all.

Count the things in each row.
Circle the same number of
things in each box.

 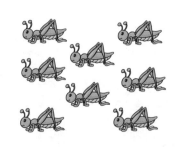

When you add two groups together the answer is called the **sum.** Count the things in each group. Write the sum.

Adding Practice

How many in all?
Write the sums.

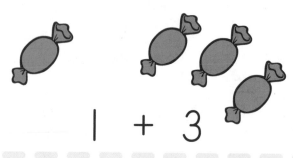 =

1 + 3

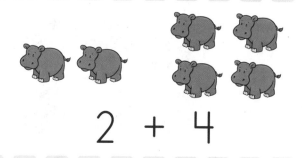 =

2 + 4

 =

4 + 4

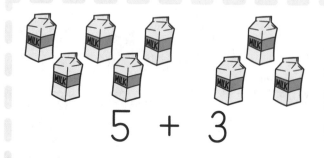 =

5 + 3

How many in all?
Write the sums.

 =

1 + 5

3 + 4

 =

3 + 5

 =

5 + 4

How many in all?
Write the sums.

$1 + 4$ =

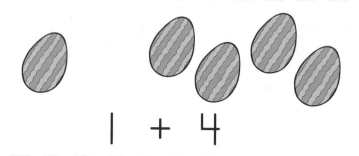

$6 + 2$ =

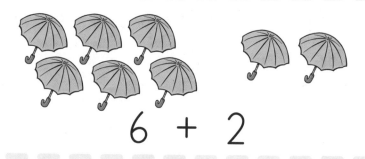

$4 + 5$ =

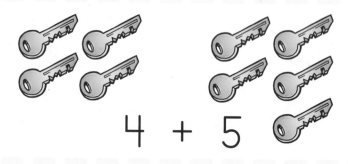

$2 + 5$ =

How many in all? Write the sums.

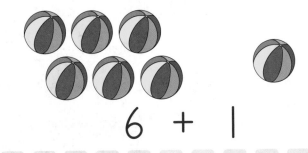

6 + 1 =

2 + 5 =

1 + 6 =

6 + 3 =

Add and write the sums.

 +  =

0 + 1 =

+ 🍎🍎 = 🍎🍎

0 + 2 =

+ 🍎🍎🍎 = 🍎🍎🍎

0 + 6 =

0 + 3 =

+ 🍎🍎🍎🍎 = 🍎🍎🍎🍎

0 + 7 =

0 + 4 =

0 + 8 =

+ 🍎🍎🍎🍎🍎 = 🍎🍎🍎🍎🍎

0 + 9 =

0 + 5 =

0 + 10 =

Add and write the sums.

☆ + ☆ = ☆☆

1 + 1 = ☐

★ + ★★ = ★★★

1 + 2 = ☐

★ + ★★★ = ★★★★

1 + 3 = ☐

1 + 6 = ☐

★ + ★★★★ = ★★★★★

1 + 4 = ☐

1 + 7 = ☐

1 + 8 = ☐

★ + ★★★★★ = ★★★★★★

1 + 5 = ☐

1 + 9 = ☐

1 + 10 = ☐

+ =

Add and write the sums.

2 + 1 =

 + =

2 + 2 =

 + =

2 + 3 =

2 + 6 =

 + =

2 + 7 =

2 + 4 =

2 + 8 =

 + =

2 + 9 =

2 + 5 =

2 + 10 =

Add and write the sums.

 + =

3 + 1 =

 + 🤍🤍 = 🤍🤍🤍 🤍🤍

3 + 2 =

🤍🤍🤍 + 🤍🤍🤍 = 🤍🤍🤍 🤍🤍🤍

3 + 3 =

3 + 6 =

 + =

3 + 4 =

3 + 7 =

3 + 8 =

 + =

3 + 9 =

3 + 5 =

3 + 10 =

Adding with 4

$4 + 1 =$

Add and write the sums.

$4 + 2 =$

$4 + 3 =$

$4 + 6 =$

$4 + 7 =$

$4 + 4 =$

$4 + 8 =$

$4 + 9 =$

$4 + 5 =$

$4 + 10 =$

Add and write the sums.

5 + 1 =

5 + 2 =

5 + 3 =

5 + 4 =

5 + 5 =

5 + 6 =

5 + 7 =

5 + 8 =

5 + 9 =

5 + 10 =

Add. Find and circle the numbers in the picture.

0 + 1 =   3 + 3 =

2 + 2 =   1 + 1 =

4 + 3 =   5 + 5 =

3 + 6 =   1 + 2 =

1 + 4 =   4 + 4 =

Add and write the sums.

🏁🏁🏁 + 🏁 = 🏁🏁🏁🏁

6 + 1 =

🏁🏁🏁🏁🏁🏁 + 🏁🏁 = 🏁🏁🏁🏁🏁🏁🏁🏁

6 + 2 =

🏁🏁🏁🏁🏁🏁 + 🏁🏁🏁 = 🏁🏁🏁🏁🏁🏁🏁🏁🏁

6 + 3 =

🏁🏁🏁🏁🏁🏁 + 🏁🏁🏁🏁 = 🏁🏁🏁🏁🏁🏁🏁🏁🏁🏁

6 + 4 =

🏁🏁🏁🏁🏁🏁 + 🏁🏁🏁🏁🏁 = 🏁🏁🏁🏁🏁🏁🏁🏁🏁🏁🏁

6 + 5 =

6 + 6 =

6 + 7 =

6 + 8 =

6 + 9 =

6 + 10 =

17

Add and write the sums.

🌼🌼🌼 + 🌼 = 🌼🌼🌼🌼

7 + 1 = ____

🌼🌼🌼 + 🌼🌼 = 🌼🌼🌼🌼🌼

7 + 2 = ____

🌼🌼🌼 + 🌼🌼🌼 = 🌼🌼🌼🌼🌼🌼

7 + 3 = ____

🌼🌼🌼 + 🌼🌼🌼🌼 = 🌼🌼🌼🌼🌼🌼🌼

7 + 4 = ____

🌼🌼🌼 + 🌼🌼🌼🌼🌼 = 🌼🌼🌼🌼🌼🌼🌼🌼

7 + 5 = ____

7 + 6 = ____

7 + 7 = ____

7 + 8 = ____

7 + 9 = ____

7 + 10 = ____

 + =

Add and write the sums.

$8 + 1 =$

 + =

$8 + 2 =$

 + =

$8 + 3 =$

$8 + 6 =$

$8 + 7 =$

 + =

$8 + 4 =$

$8 + 8 =$

$8 + 9 =$

$8 + 5 =$

$8 + 10 =$

Add and write the sums.

9 + 1 =

9 + 2 =

9 + 3 =

9 + 4 =

9 + 5 =

9 + 6 =

9 + 7 =

9 + 8 =

9 + 9 =

9 + 10 =

+ =

$10 + 1 =$

  =

$10 + 2 =$

$10 + 3 =$

  =

$10 + 4 =$

 + =

$10 + 5 =$

Add and write the sums.

$10 + 6 =$

$10 + 7 =$

$10 + 8 =$

$10 + 9 =$

$10 + 10 =$

Add and write the sums.

$1 + 1 =$ $5 + 8 =$

$1 + 2 =$ $6 + 4 =$ $3 + 9 =$

$1 + 3 =$ $2 + 4 =$ $3 + 5 =$

$1 + 4 =$ $2 + 5 =$ $4 + 1 =$

$1 + 5 =$ $3 + 1 =$ $4 + 2 =$

$2 + 1 =$ $3 + 2 =$ $4 + 3 =$

$9 + 1 =$ $7 + 2 =$ $6 + 2 =$

Add and write the sums.

4+4=

8+1=

9+5=

4+5=

7+3=

2+3=

5+1=

6+3=

3+7=

5+2=

2+7=

6+1=

5+3=

7+6=

4+6=

5+4=

8+4=

2+8=

5+5=

2+6=

5+6=

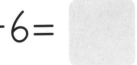

Add and write the sums.

1
+1

2
+3

8
+3

6
+3

1
+5

7
+2

2
+1

2
+4

3
+3

Add and write the sums.

5
+2

1
+4

3
+1

4
+2

5
+4

4
+3

5
+5

8
+2

Adding Without Things

Add and write the sums.

1 +1	5 +7	2 +2	7 +4	9 +5
9 +3	4 +3	6 +3	8 +6	6 +9
2 +1	3 +1	7 +7	3 +6	2 +7

Add the **ones.**

Write each sum.

$$
\begin{array}{r}
23 \\
+34 \\
\hline
\end{array}
\qquad
\begin{array}{r}
12 \\
+86 \\
\hline
\end{array}
\qquad
\begin{array}{r}
45 \\
+12 \\
\hline
\end{array}
\qquad
\begin{array}{r}
76 \\
+13 \\
\hline
\end{array}
$$

$$
\begin{array}{r}
53 \\
+36 \\
\hline
\end{array}
\qquad
\begin{array}{r}
87 \\
+12 \\
\hline
\end{array}
\qquad
\begin{array}{r}
43 \\
+16 \\
\hline
\end{array}
\qquad
\begin{array}{r}
63 \\
+35 \\
\hline
\end{array}
$$

1. $0 + 1 =$
5. $6 + 7 =$
9. $1 + 4 =$

2. $5 + 10 =$
6. $9 + 8 =$
10. $3 + 3 =$

3. $2 + 2 =$
7. $3 + 6 =$
11. $1 + 1 =$

4. $4 + 3 =$
8. $6 + 6 =$
12. $8 + 8 =$

Follow the numbers in the order of your answers to see who finds the basketball.

Answers page 1

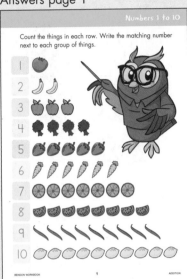

Answers page 2

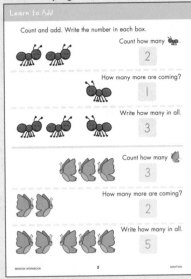

Answers page 3

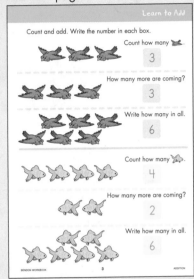

Answers page 4

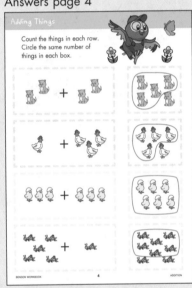

Answers page 5

Answers page 6

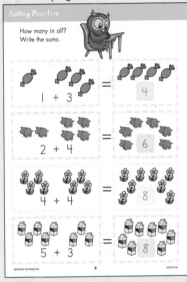

Answers page 7

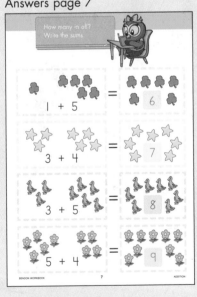

Answers page 8

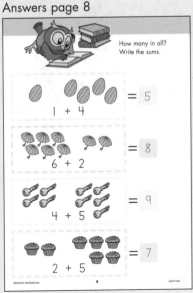

Answers page 9

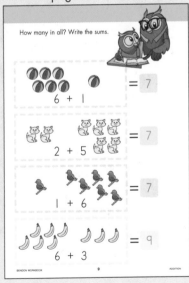

Answers page 10

Adding with 0

Add and write the sums.

$+ \; = \;$

$0 + 1 = 1$

$+ \; = \;$

$0 + 2 = 2$

$+ \; = \;$

$0 + 3 = 3$ $0 + 6 = 6$

$+ \; = \;$

$0 + 7 = 7$

$0 + 4 = 4$ $0 + 8 = 8$

$+ \; = \;$

$0 + 9 = 9$

$0 + 5 = 5$ $0 + 10 = 10$

BENDON WORKBOOK   10   ADDITION

Answers page 11

Adding with 1

Add and write the sums.

$\star + \star = \star\star$

$1 + 1 = 2$

$\star + \star\star = \star\star\star$

$1 + 2 = 3$

$\star + \star\star\star = \star\star\star\star$

$1 + 3 = 4$ $1 + 6 = 7$

$\star + \star\star\star\star = \star\star\star\star\star$

$1 + 7 = 8$

$1 + 4 = 5$ $1 + 8 = 9$

$\star + \star\star\star\star\star = \star\star\star\star\star\star$

$1 + 9 = 10$

$1 + 5 = 6$ $1 + 10 = 11$

BENDON WORKBOOK   11   ADDITION

Answers page 12

Adding with 2

$+ \; = \;$

$2 + 1 = 3$

$+ \; = \;$

$2 + 2 = 4$

$+ \; = \;$

$2 + 3 = 5$ $2 + 6 = 8$

$2 + 7 = 9$

$+ \; = \;$

$2 + 4 = 6$ $2 + 8 = 10$

$+ \; = \;$

$2 + 9 = 11$

$2 + 5 = 7$ $2 + 10 = 12$

BENDON WORKBOOK   12   ADDITION

Answers page 13

$+ \; = \;$

Add and write the sums.

$3 + 1 = 4$

$+ \; = \;$

$3 + 2 = 5$

$+ \; = \;$

$3 + 3 = 6$ $3 + 6 = 9$

$3 + 7 = 10$

$+ \; = \;$

$3 + 4 = 7$ $3 + 8 = 11$

$+ \; = \;$

$3 + 9 = 12$

$3 + 5 = 8$ $3 + 10 = 13$

BENDON WORKBOOK   13   ADDITION

Answers page 14

Adding with 4

$+ \; = \;$

$4 + 1 = 5$

$+ \; = \;$

Add and write the sums.

$4 + 2 = 6$

$+ \; = \;$

$4 + 3 = 7$ $4 + 6 = 10$

$4 + 7 = 11$

$+ \; = \;$

$4 + 4 = 8$ $4 + 8 = 12$

$4 + 9 = 13$

$+ \; = \;$

$4 + 5 = 9$ $4 + 10 = 14$

BENDON WORKBOOK   14   ADDITION

Answers page 15

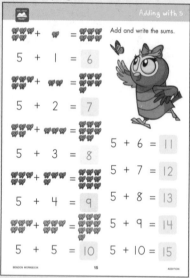

Adding with 5

$+ \; = \;$

Add and write the sums.

$5 + 1 = 6$

$+ \; = \;$

$5 + 2 = 7$

$+ \; = \;$

$5 + 3 = 8$ $5 + 6 = 11$

$5 + 7 = 12$

$+ \; = \;$

$5 + 4 = 9$ $5 + 8 = 13$

$5 + 9 = 14$

$5 + 5 = 10$ $5 + 10 = 15$

BENDON WORKBOOK   15   ADDITION

Answers page 16

Hidden Numbers!

Add. Find and circle the numbers in the picture.

$0 + 1 = 1$ $3 + 3 = 6$

$2 + 2 = 4$ $1 + 1 = 2$

$4 + 3 = 7$ $5 + 5 = 10$

$3 + 6 = 9$ $1 + 2 = 3$

$1 + 4 = 5$ $4 + 4 = 8$

BENDON WORKBOOK   16   ADDITION

Answers page 17

Adding with 6

$+ \; = \;$

$6 + 1 = 7$

$+ \; = \;$

$6 + 2 = 8$

$+ \; = \;$

$6 + 6 = 12$

$6 + 3 = 9$ $6 + 7 = 13$

$+ \; = \;$

$6 + 8 = 14$

$6 + 4 = 10$ $6 + 9 = 15$

$+ \; = \;$

$6 + 5 = 11$ $6 + 10 = 16$

BENDON WORKBOOK   17   ADDITION

Answers page 18

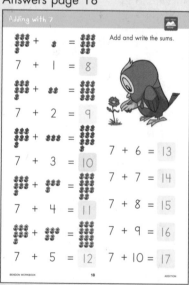

Adding with 7

$+ \; = \;$

Add and write the sums.

$7 + 1 = 8$

$+ \; = \;$

$7 + 2 = 9$

$+ \; = \;$

$7 + 6 = 13$

$7 + 3 = 10$ $7 + 7 = 14$

$7 + 8 = 15$

$7 + 4 = 11$ $7 + 9 = 16$

$+ \; = \;$

$7 + 5 = 12$ $7 + 10 = 17$

BENDON WORKBOOK   18   ADDITION

Answers page 19

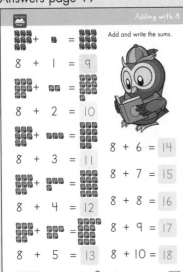

Adding with 8

Add and write the sums.

8 + 1 = 9
8 + 2 = 10
8 + 3 = 11
8 + 4 = 12
8 + 5 = 13

8 + 6 = 14
8 + 7 = 15
8 + 8 = 16
8 + 9 = 17
8 + 10 = 18

Answers page 20

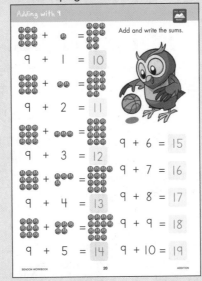

Adding with 9

Add and write the sums.

9 + 1 = 10
9 + 2 = 11
9 + 3 = 12
9 + 4 = 13
9 + 5 = 14

9 + 6 = 15
9 + 7 = 16
9 + 8 = 17
9 + 9 = 18
9 + 10 = 19

Answers page 21

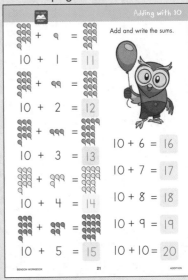

Adding with 10

Add and write the sums.

10 + 1 = 11
10 + 2 = 12
10 + 3 = 13
10 + 4 = 14
10 + 5 = 15

10 + 6 = 16
10 + 7 = 17
10 + 8 = 18
10 + 9 = 19
10 + 10 = 20

Answers page 22

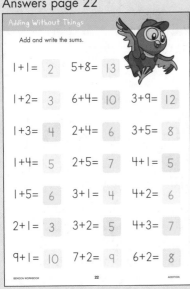

Adding Without Things

Add and write the sums.

1+1= 2   5+8= 13
1+2= 3   6+4= 10   3+9= 12
1+3= 4   2+4= 6   3+5= 8
1+4= 5   2+5= 7   4+1= 5
1+5= 6   3+1= 4   4+2= 6
2+1= 3   3+2= 5   4+3= 7
9+1= 10   7+2= 9   6+2= 8

Answers page 23

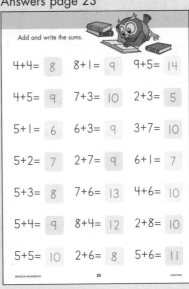

Add and write the sums.

4+4= 8   8+1= 9   9+5= 14
4+5= 9   7+3= 10   2+3= 5
5+1= 6   6+3= 9   3+7= 10
5+2= 7   2+7= 9   6+1= 7
5+3= 8   7+6= 13   4+6= 10
5+4= 9   8+4= 12   2+8= 10
5+5= 10   2+6= 8   5+6= 11

Answers page 24

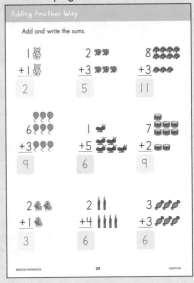

Adding Another Way

Add and write the sums.

1   2   8
+1   +3   +3
2   5   11

6   1   7
+3   +5   +2
9   6   9

2   2   3
+1   +4   +3
3   6   6

Answers page 25

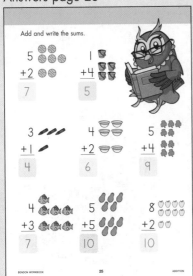

Add and write the sums.

5   1
+2   +4
7   5

3   4   5
+1   +2   +4
4   6   9

4   5   8
+3   +5   +2
7   10   10

Answers page 26

Adding Without Things

Add and write the sums.

1   5   2   7   9
+1   +7   +2   +4   +5
2   12   4   11   14

9   4   6   8   6
+3   +3   +3   +6   +9
12   7   9   14   15

2   3   7   3   2
+1   +1   +7   +6   +7
3   4   14   9   9

Answers page 27

Challenge! Adding Ones and Tens

TENS ONES
23
+34
7

TENS ONES
23
+34
57

Add the ones.   Then add the tens.

Write each sum.

23   12   45   76
+34   +86   +12   +13
57   98   57   89

53   87   43   63
+36   +12   +16   +35
89   99   59   98

Fun Family Activities

These activities will provide review of the concepts
explored on the workbook pages.

1. Adding in the Park

Provide the child with many opportunities to count groups of things and add
the groups together. For example, when you are at the park, count how many
children are on the swings and how many children are on the slide. Add the two
groups together to find how many children in all.

2. Playing Card Addition

Use a deck of playing cards without the face cards. Set the deck in a pile on
the table. Ask the child to draw two cards and add the numbers together. If the
answer is correct, the child keeps the two cards and draws two more. When a
wrong answer is given, the cards are returned to the bottom of the deck and play
advances to the player to the left. Continue playing until all the cards are gone.
The player with the most cards wins. Reshuffle and play again.

3. Make Your Own Story Problems

Start a story problem and have the child finish the problem. Then change places
and let the child tell the story. A story you might tell is: "I went to the store and
bought six apples and three oranges. How many pieces of fruit did I buy?" Try
telling other addition stories.

4. Reward Stickers

Use reward stickers to celebrate a job well done. You or the child can choose
when to place a sticker on a specific page. Use a sticker as a reward when the
child completes a page that requires extra care or is a little more difficult. The
child can choose to place stickers on pages he or she is proud of completing.

Answers page 28

Illustrations by: Greg Hardin